LOVE AINT

...

Man vs Heart

Derrick Ballard Jr.

Co-Authored By
Berlinda White

Love Aint... Man vs Heart
Copyright © 2014 by Derrick Ballard

All rights reserved. No part of this book may be reproduced or transmitted in any form or by any means without written permission from the author.

ISBN 978-1495485145

By Kreative Orkrestra Novels

Chapters

Dedication .... *v*

Introduction .... *vi*

Chapter 1: Opening Scene *1*

Chapter 2: How it all started *4*

Chapter 3: Degrees of separation *12*

Chapter 4: Fresh *18*

Chapter 5: Nobody's perfect *26*

Chapter 6: Girls, Girls, Girls *37*

Chapter 7: Growing fast *43*

Chapter 8: Dreams *50*

Chapter 9: For the wrong reason *64*

Chapter 10: Tempos, beats & creativity *74*

Chapter 11: Flip a coin *78*

Chapter 11.1: Third eye- just blind *84*

Chapter 12: Unconditionally yours *90*

Chapter 13: Closing scene *97*

"Never surrender, it's all about the faith you got: don't ever stop, just push it 'till you hit the top and if you drop, at least you know you gave your all to be true to you, that way you can never fall"

"Did you hear about the rose that grew from a crack in the concrete? Proving nature's laws wrong, it learned to walk without having feet. Funny, it seems to by keeping it's dreams; it learned to breathe fresh air. Long live the rose that grew from concrete when no one else even cared."

-Tupac Shakur

Dedication

I would like to dedicate this piece to all of my family and friends. The concept for this novel came into place as I came to a crossroads in my life. I want the world to know my story. It shall inspire everyone to accomplish his or her dreams and keep faith alive.

Thank You: GOD, Derrick "Zion" III, my mother, Derrick Sr.,Mark, Dorothy Searcy, Lavia, Sherry, Rashad, Mark Devonte', Samaree, Jocelyn, Ashton, Primas Simpson, Keyon, Timothy, James, A.Rose. Libra, Marnita, Kim, Sharon, Uncle Donald, Berlinda, Willie Brank, Meat, Kevin, TJ, Ray Ray, Chip, Mary, Linda, Andre, Sanchez, Trina, Wendy, Libra, Jorel, Brittany, Ivory/Shyne, Synii, Nyelle, Ivory, Deonte', Darryl, Sweat Da Track, Manny, Soupe, Ed, G Roe. Ashley, Teddy Riley, Brian, Hash,Prime, Astro, Keenan, Matthew, Connie, Cynthia, G & Ashanti (MatureHeartsLL). If I forgot your name, I apologize.

Rest In Peace: Ron "The Future" Brown, Lo (No Mercy), Jazzy, Throwback, Angela, Aunt Jeanette, Camouflage, Aunt Sarah, Willie, Slim, Phat & Red

Introduction

I met June online, after he had recently been in my area doing interviews for a video shoot and his iDYMES Magazine. I thought of him as a very interprising and intelligent young man. It was something very alluring about his soul.

I wanted to talk to him more and ask a million questions. I am the type of person whom is always curious and wants to learn as much in life as possible. I wanted to see where all of this light was coming from. I often want to lift people even higher than what they are. I am a proud supporter. I never have the hater or jealous mode blinking it isn't in me or part of my characteristic.

I always have the side joke that I think that there is at least one good book in every angelic soul on this earth. As I began to talk to June I told him that he definitely needed to write a book and share his story with the world. What excited me was where he was and the journey he had mad to now. I wanted him to share that, knowing that it would surely inspire someone else. I thank June for his story. There is much more to tell he is such an outstanding gentleman. Join me in thanking him for sharing.

Berlinda White

When one can find a man
That opens
His heart truly
There is a gage that changes in the wind
And all of the contents of the world
Begin to spill as if precious jewels
A mans heart holds the key to all things
Be not weary of the truths
Accept like the greatest gifts
Of an invisible soul
-L.A. Sincere-

Chapter 1
Opening Scene

I'm sitting here, flipping through the channels, in a dark toasty room. There are no bells jing-a-linging here, no flashing lights no carols. Its Christmas Eve, so everybody is so excited about tomorrow. Yea, everybody but me, I see no point in being excited. While surfing I see shows like "Love &Hip-Hop" and many other reality shows. The people on these shows seem to amuse me.

They fight and argue about the dumbest shit in the world. I see these men and women that don't appreciate the state of being monogamous in this era. Yet they scream keep me I'm yours, I love you. My question though, why the fuck am I watching this or television period and all of its silly programs. My heart feels like a six hundred pound man has stepped on it. More like the feeling of desperation, the feeling like a kid who has lost their best friend. I tumble and fall though I am sitting still, wrecked though not inside a car.

My turmoil may also be compared to a deep fall from the heavens. I never thought in a million years I would be sitting here feeling like this over a woman! Yea, I said it, a woman! Those that know me may not take me seriously, but I guess it's my turn to wander through this agony. The night's mood doesn't make me feel any better. The night feels somber, crisp, cold, dark and impaling.

Everyone is asleep, the lights are extremely low, the fireplace is lit and a nigga is sitting here alone. I can't do anything but think about all the relationships I've been through in the past. I am starting to believe that I deserve this. Who knows maybe I do . In my past I've been with my share of females.

Lust was the reason why I wanted them, after we had sex, I would stop calling or just plain found a reason to not fuck with them anymore. Hey I'm just being honest. Yeah I know you don't expect that from brothers like me! Well I'm about to give it to you raw. Being faithful and committed to just one person was never an option for me. I kind of figured that I wouldn't be a good boyfriend because I couldn't keep my ass still.

I was so confused, chasing and never keeping. I had started to believe that someone put a root on me. You know that voodoo that you do. What went around is surely coming back at the moment. It's a mystery to me how each woman felt after I left them behind. Having feelings for someone and to lie to them seems kind of harsh. I know I'd be the last person they wanted to talk to.

Its been said that man will have his heart broken three times before he finds his soul mate. Well ok I am hoping this is just a theory. It's a theory that certainly won't apply to me in the future. For like two weeks now, I haven't had an appetite nor have I been in any sort of good mood. I can probably even say I have lost weight. I am not looking my best, I'm looking weak, hollow and like I am going through something.

Hell I feel like drinking some Hen & Coke, you know what I'm saying can't have these emotions displayed. You all are probably thinking this nigga is crazy. Well I think I am personally. As I sit and think my rage is building up because Shorty hasn't even called me all day. Questions have been flashing through my mind, one after another continuously. You don't even want to know what I was thinking now.

What is she doing? Who is she with? My thoughts are everywhere right now. Why would she even put me through this sort of pain, it's consuming me. All of this is crazy to me and I am getting no relief what so ever.

Hopefully she is doing this just to prove a point. It's getting to be very overwhelming. I'm so far behind on my work. I've deleted my face book account and turned my phone off. It seemed as if everything reminded me of her. I'm reminded of her skin, her scent, her beauty. I'm thinking to myself "Fuck that bitch" but I know dam well that's not how I really feel. There is no telling how long this is going to last. I'm praying not long because I'm ready to eat.

Chapter 2

How It All Started

The year was 1987; I was conceived on the Island of Oahu Island, for those that don't know. It's located on Honolulu Island. The same hospital President Obama was born in. From what I've been told my father was the proudest man in the world when I was born.

He made sure I was fed and didn't want anyone to pick me up. If anyone picked me up it was him. Bouncing me around like a proud papa. You couldn't steal that moment from him; deny me or him those moments or tides. He cradled me like those moments would last forever yet they didn't. What fills up a man's heart often deflates it. Well that only lasted for six months, my father left my mother and I behind. He moved back to Atlanta to be with another woman. Little do they know, by him leaving, it will affect me for the rest of my life. I believe that this situation made my mother adjust her feelings for men. My father's absence tainted my relationship with my mother some type of way.

It was a lot to take, on yet she still managed to make things happen. I know when she looks at me, she see my father. Wow, all of those strong features just popping out at ya. If I only understood back then what is so damn apparent to me now. She had so much strength and instilled it within me for survival.

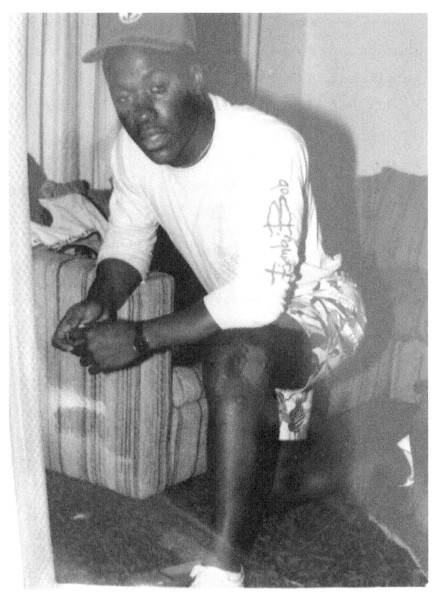

(This is my father Derrick Ballard Sr. in 1987)

This short dark complexioned lady was a "beast". You hear me? Being aggressive made her a force to be wrecking with. In 1991 my mom met her future husband. This was kind of awkward for me because I wasn't used to having a man with and around her. Just thinking about it now, I didn't know what she saw in someone that was five years younger than she was. Being that she never had been attracted to light complexioned males, or males that were younger than her, this was something that was very significant.

My stepfather was suave, the Billy Dee type, he had a lot of game and was laying it all on the court. Before they were married the couple used to "break up" to "make-up" all of the time. I was too young to understand back then what was going on, but I understand now what that was. It seems kind of funny. Hearing a grown man beg for forgiveness from outside the door was quite hilarious being in the military didn't make it any better, mom pulled rank on him whenever she needed to in those private quarters.

As a child growing up I was very mild mannered and obedient Solely because I knew if I was going to act up I was going to get my ass whooped. When I messed up my mother made sure she got that respect, there wasn't any if ands and buts about it.

By no means you all, am I exploiting my lovely mother. I am just pointing out the many defining moments to make my point clear. Ok!

Around age six or seven, I developed an instinct of trying to keep my moms happy and to be a "noble child". I wasn't good at first. After a few ass whoopings and having only two ninja turtles left, my mouthpiece had to be on point. Yes. Sir you were crazy if you thought you were going to get me to say the wrong thing in front of my mother.

At the age of twelve I started yearning for something. To be honest I had no idea of what it was. There were moments when nothing seemed to satisfy. I craved and longed for something I had no way of understanding at that age. If roaming vagabonds felt like this, my difference was that, I just wasn't a traveler at the time.

To go back a little for you, when people think of paradise so many things occur to them. The paradise moments in your heart then you also have the places people long to go to. Being born there in Hawaii and my father leaving so early left a scar I couldn't even describe. His leaving shaped me in ways I wouldn't be able to claim until much later. I saw drifting beautiful crystal sands, breezy whipped palm trees shaking for me, and long tailed lizards running all over the place. Those lizards acted like we were in their territory, invading their space. I know naturally we were kind of burgeoning on their habitat. Those young memories will never fail me.

I became aware of different places that I floated to, holding tight to my few toys. Ever so often as my mother and I had to depart ways, as she would go on duty, I would feel a complete emptiness. Different cities many different travels, I looked and was learning all the while. When I was around age three or four I lived with my Grandmother for a while. My mother was stationed in San Diego, California at the time. My grandmother actually raised me until mom was stable. She was making a better life for her and me. That's something that women do all the time for themselves and their children, Make a better life. While men run off not from their partners but their feelings of how to cope through this emotion as a man.

I can remember one day, mom had one of her friends drive me from Atlanta to where she was at. Being only about three I didn't know what was going on. I was in the back seat, sitting in between luggage. I had my Sunday best on, lost in between the shadows of day and night. The ride took about 3 days. When we finally got there, I remember seeing my mother and I was really excited. This feeling never left when I would see my mother after long episodes of not being together.

(Mommy & I. When I was two years old.)

Growing up, being fresh was not a problem for me, mom always had me in the fly Jordan's and kept a roof over my head.

Yet I can tell you there are moments when something was strange off key. Ladies, ladies don't the little people in your life aren't picking up on everything from an early age. If I fell and scraped my knee I found my own band aids. Whenever I had a tummy ache or wasn't feeling good there was no one there to soothe me. Mom loved her little man but she wasn't always there.

As sentimental as the shit may sound, the emotional or motherly connection wasn't present. I've noticed all and had to accept her ways. Of course at the time I didn't understand the logic. I just knew I wanted my mommy. This was evident. I focused on it in an assuming way. You all know many times you can't tell what's in a man's heart unless he tells you.

As I started to engage myself into new areas as hormones raged, I gained a strong love for music. I developed something to control my uneasiness, caress them emotional demons inside me. Oh it seemed as if I had learners of "life" from the songs I enjoyed listening to. Music answered a multiple slew of questions for me; it drew me away from my reality. My surroundings pulled me in as I grew. You may have said my world was growing toxic but I rattled my stride with caution. After a while I started to notice that I wasn't her little boy anymore. Me my mother and step father weren't on really good terms, we never saw eye to eye on a few things.

Jumping from being the little man cradled in his arms to being a full-grown man. I recollect on how life's changed. What all did it take to get here and the moments that became a part of this movement, "The life and times of me Derrick Ballard Jr.". Just this year we vowed to make things right. Now they have been married over twenty years and have two kids together. Now this man isn't the one that helped procreate me, yet he is the one I also am supposed to acknowledge as a dad. I believe the saying "you are a product of your parents". That is exactly why I was so cold sometimes lifeless. I was never the affectionate type or rarely cried about anything yet you can bet I handle emotion totally different than you'd expect.

"LOVE FLOWER"

Love is a vine that is rooted within, how it grows depends on the type of soil and climate it is placed in. the stem of this plant can be so strong that it can adapt to any weather conditions, but the slightest thing can make it wither away.

Chapter 3

Degrees of Separation

Nobody wants to be a damn clone, some sort of robot or "copy cats", and no, definitely not even me. Ladies, one of the main things that separate our sexes is that men often know how to admire what they see. If a man can learn from any thing he see's he builds upon it, makes changes personally, financially or even spiritually. We may not even totally understand the concept yet we will try. We are very analytical, give us a dam puzzle we know we can solve it without they're being any view of a beginning or end. We simply walk into chaos and think we can define everything. We often sit quietly and reserved solving puzzles, prying chains, and then unlocking cubes in our head, without touching on the main facts.

We don't like to show an ounce of emotion. Let me change that statement, hell we don't like to show a milli miniscule, get your magnifying glass, barely am I breathing eye dropper of emotion. Yet you scream for so much of us to be given to you yes we want to give you US, without giving you US fully, thoroughly or even partially. We don't want you taking what we feel and using it against us, throwing it round like our thoughts, feelings are nothing. We cut form the same cloth baby girl yet we are stitched a different way. The stitching can make a huge difference in how we perceive life.

So when you get to acting like we creatures from a different planet, hey it's not that extreme, yet respect, the code of the DNA is slightly different. Even women who have a slight quiet element about them, you know the ones that know how to shut up and respect your dam space, without going on and on. These ladies even are different. Some of you sister's, constantly go to war, verbal destruction, ripping at us with a barrage of insanity. We not going to dam cope with that. Letting you follow us around a few hours let alone a lifetime you all must be dam crazy.

Every woman who thinks she can be cooperative enough to get the one then show it is not fooling anyone. When I say co-operative, I mean saying yes to everything, not fussing, yelling or demanding anything. Listen men will say just about anything to get what they want. Yet unless you have this vibe, connection we feel, yet can't put our finger on. Like, the entire galaxy slapping us upside the head, saying "Derrick she the one". We don't just give in like that. We fear showing you Shorty that we melting inside, falling and want to sling them arms around you and hold you forever. We don't know what it is, that makes us not want to tell the truth and be free with our feelings. Fear I guess fear of failure, fear of her laughing saying, okay but you not hot boy. Sit down somewhere I'm off to the next one.

We know we have done it to women many times, broken more hearts than we can remember. Caused emotional stress to more women we can name. Yet it all starts way before the date, before the hello, before the glance. It's a personal flaw, a flag that's thrown before we even hit the football field. My dismay and non-believing started when my mother left me alone. I couldn't connect with her as I should. When I felt she wouldn't be there and bring that feeling of safety comfort that I needed when I needed it.

You may say well my mom was always there. My partner never been through that, he and his father always got along. Yet ladies what you don't understand is that we all have been molded we are not clay and were not the first Adam and Eve blown from sand. We are etched, carved completed by every marking making, of what we see and go through from being born to adolescence to adulthood. We may not all get it right, right away yet we try and sometimes you have just as many flames and darts shooting from your past and we act like to trails of lava just flowing from a volcano. We collide, slow down, stop and just harden like an impasse.

Do your best to give everything time, don't expect so much so soon. I even notice how many elements carved me into the makings of me. Now, some meant nothing in the past yet as I became a man I learned to be more faithful and prayerful knowing

God had a way carved just for me. It wasn't meant for anyone else at all. Our destiny was set from before we were ever born. I know there is certain magic in places, people, and dates.

I was born on March 14th the same day as the great Albert Einstein Theoretical Physicist and also the Great Musical composer Quincy Jones. My ambitions won't let me sleep sometimes because I grind so hard trying to get things done. You can say ambition and drive runs in the family. One of my relatives is Jimmy Gates of the group Silk, you know with all the hits like "Meeting in my Bedroom, Please Don't Go, Lose Control and Freak Me (baby)" yeah the ladies seem to love those hits especially the last one. I am also related to NFL Defensive End former player Christian Ballard he played for the Minnesota Vikings he abruptly retired last year.

If you happen to be a true music lover then just maybe the Surname Ballard sounds familiar to you. Well incase you don't know here is the story. My grandfather Willie Ballard and Jesse Lambert were adopted brothers. The Ballard family adopted them. Jessie's Original surname was Lambert they changed it to Ballard after adopting him. Jesse's daughter is the famous Florence Ballard; you know one of thee original Supremes out of "Motown" Records in Detroit, which sang with Diana Ross and Mary Wells.

Jesse's grandmother was killed that's when he was adopted. He was living in Bessemer, Alabama Jesse was musically inclined, a local musician he fell for Florence's mother, and she was from Rosetta, Mississippi. The family moved to Detroit in 1929, the Ballard's had 13 kids, Florence Ballard was thee eighth child. Jessie influenced his daughters singing and taught her songs, frequently had her singing while he accompanied on guitar.

Hank Ballard was Florence Ballard's cousin; he also had lived in Bessemer, Alabama as a young boy. They described Hank's music as a little of everything country, jazz, bluesy, country and rock and roll. Hank was responsible for the hit the "Twist" done by Chubby Checker, he was responsible for many more hits and he even was a part of the group, the Midnighter's and later as a solo artist

Just the vibe of greatness in your lineage can provoke you to do many great things. My mother is an Eastern Star and my father was a Mason. I follow along the same path now that I have more discipline in my life. I often watched others in my neighborhood, not have any sort of strength or discipline when they knew we had to listen to the elders and their perspectives. Heck what the hell am I talking about; certainly I didn't follow a positive path from the beginning.

Chapter 4
Fresh

I always noticed sexy people and sexy people noticed me. To tell you the truth I was girl crazy since about the first grade. Of course we stayed in different places military housing etc. But I was really fly, always looking like I stepped off a magazine. I knew they were saying is this young kid a male model, okay now, haters were even checking me back then. My swag was always on point, mom made sure of that. I loved new fresh clothes couldn't wait to break em out.

Really I couldn't even wait to get to school to see some of those super fine girls that I was checking out. I was macking from the moment I got into the front door of the school. I gave them those come here glances. I just about had a teacher or two mesmerized, they even were being flirtatious back and forth. I gladly always helped with anything; a nice looking teacher would ask me to. Some had that body, you know banging so hard, when she walked, you thought it was an earthquake shaking from side to side. I used to notice everything, from the hair, to the clothes, to the make up. Can't say I didn't learn that if women had it going on, they stood a chance of getting what they wanted. A ten can make it further than a two or three. Noticing that it helped me with the line of work I'm into today.

My first celebrity crush was on Monica. You couldn't tell me anything. I thought she was perfect. I had her posters all over my wall I even had them tacked on my ceiling above my bed. Oh yeah I was addicted to Black Men's magazines like King Magazine as a youngster, I used to cut the pictures out and put them all over my wall in my room. My room was my comfort zone reading magazines was my way of motivating myself, so that I could have some peace.

There were several young ladies I flirted with back and forth. They had the mysterious shy smiles, alluring voices and I followed. But dam I thought I could move on too bigger and better things. Well I won't lie its not that I felt super secure with those girls, they weren't just so easy they were going to let me lay them down. Once I went down to the beauty shop where my mother was it had its array of different women there, all different types of classes o sexy ladies. I practically had a hard on when I walked in the door. Some were smiling and reading books or magazines, many were constantly talking loud and gossiping, I was like dam as I listened to the stories I heard up in there.

One particular lady caught my eye though. It was as if the room slowed down and everything was like slow motion, I couldn't keep my eyes off of her. Her smile was so sexy and her hips were calling my name. This woman charmed me like a snake coming up out of a basket. Did I have a flute magically playing it luring her close to me? I'm going to call her "Cookie", Cookie talked with me, we often laughed when I crossed he path. She was so seductive she asked me about, how many ladies I was breaking hearts? I told her not that many, she smiled, and told me that she thought my smile was a knock out and that I looked like I had some strong hands. Hmm, hell these hands surely wanted to caress that damn body. Cookie gave me her number she had started, speaking about how she wanted to see what I had in me. Well hot dam, I surely wanted to show her. My manhood couldn't calm down when she was near; the serpent was ready to hiss at Eve. We made plans to get together one day.

I was fifteen at the time and yes she was a thirty eight year old. I snuck her into my moms house, oh yeah it was outrageous. She did things to me that blew my mind, and in return I gave her some of this chocolate thunder. I was a virgin at the time but the sex was mid blowing. How could I possibly back that up with other young ladies? Let's just say I learned a few tricks indeed that day. This guy earned several stars.

I would stand by my locker trying to make a few transactions and girls were constantly, trying to pass me notes and hold conversations. I was pretty popular at school for more than one reason, let me rephrase that I was quite popular with the ladies. They were ready to submit and give their love to me. First of all ladies, just because we have sex doesn't mean we are a couple, that we even fall in love with you. Sex is just what it is 97% of the time, its just plain old sex. Ladies you get your emotions attached so quickly, even before sex you have even claimed us as mates. No, No, No that's far too early, you names and faces not personalities or habits. This is how your hearts get broken so easily. You never bother to invest time into a relationship. Meaning did you take the time to hang out with this brother long enough, before you started dating him to even see was he the right one. You can't be angry at us for banging you and running off, you opened up.

Ladies you open up your heart, your soul and your legs all at once and expect that because you serve up a brother that he is so pleased he is staying. A man can get that any place so you need to make sure a relationship develops and that he is worthy of you opening up your legs for him. The guys couldn't stand me at school. The only reason they wanted to be bothered with me is because I made the hottest CD's and sold them out of my locker and sold that weed for them to get blazed up with.

I regret now treating some of the beautiful ladies just as packages, but you have got to always remember you are not able to just blame the other party for being responsible and breaking your heart, dam, you must be responsible for your own heart. If you sit it out there be strong enough to handle any repercussions that may happen to occur. I used to lie and tell somewhat they wanted to hear in order to have that moment of passion, at the same time I couldn't even believe how easy it was to just have a chick give me what I wanted without even saying a word.

While growing up I was heavily into sports, it was a great release of frustration and energy. I played baseball, basketball, football and I ran track. I knew everybody and everybody knew me. Sometimes it's a good thing to be known as the "go to" guy supplying their needs. I learned what I knew from brothers on the block. The streets played a heavy role in my life. They were my fathers. I felt like I had no choice but to play the game like that. There is always a choice in the matter; you may think there isn't there is.

My morals came from my mother, but my logic and tactical state of mind came from the male figures I was around. It wasn't like I was some gangster but I did a little this and that to get by. My partners were the ones living that hard life and almost losing their lives. I can remember one day, we were in the bleachers talking and my partners were discussing the future and all of a sudden some of my partner's enemies hollered out his name and pulled something that looked like a gun out, I jumped up and grabbed my knapsack and ran as hard as I could jumping fences in neighborhoods and cutting corners till I saw or heard no one behind me. I got separated from my friend but he ended up letting me know he was okay.

When I got home I was fussed at of course because I reeked with the scent of weed and I paced back and forth in my room like something was wrong. I just wanted a moment of peace in my house. Our home had its own turmoil and issues; its bad when you can't even have a sense of peace in your own household. Sometimes it seemed as if prayers didn't do any good. Yet in the long run now I know that they did.

Without a father being there I still felt myself growing and learning. Street knowledge its not like that everyday knowledge, it takes you to an entire different level. I would just get intuitions about certain people and steer clear of their paths, knowing that they seemed like some extra dangerous motherfuckers. Certain incidents would immediately be a red flag to me. It was like I would have a moment of déjà vu. Shit have I been here in this exact moment before, is this some type of instant replay. Moments like that saved my life, because they forced me to abort certain stupid situations.

The only thing I couldn't escape from was my disoriented family. They have been beefing and arguing since as long as I could remember. My family is totally dysfunctional; there are several things that occurred a while back that has divided each other. It's been going on now for over thirty years. This had me inspired to try and reconcile the family and also start my own.

When you have room full of people that just can't come together it leaves a deep wound. I've been hurting for a long time as if someone has poured salt in several open wounds. Individuals are always so hard and uncooperative. Everyone is always blaming someone one else pointing fingers and causing more chaos; nobody takes into consideration what they have done to keep the situation the way it is. It never even matters who started it. Shit, just who in the world, that's in the mix, is going to untangle this?

We have got to learn how to move forward and do better in this society.

Chapter 5
Nobody's Perfect

My parents were young when they conceived me. Nobody's to blame. In this world things happen and we just follow the course not even knowing some win, some lose, yet you don't have to follow the blues. Pride gets in our way all of the time, like a fucked up piece of shit, if you run slap into it on a sidewalk you are going to try your best and kick it off your shoe, though you can't just throw it and not be left with something nasty that lingers behind. No matter in what form it may come in, its there and you got to notice that shit.

Out of respect for the people in your life you sometimes want to change and not leave them remnants, just show what would it, truly be like if we cleaned things up the right way. Why in life do we lie so much, and play so many games. I didn't no more realize the harm I did to others, no more than the damage that was done to me. I think about the moments like when I slept with this one or that one and never answered a never phone call from them or gave them a glance. I was too busy to be pleasing people. I only wanted to please me. You can tell sisters how it really is and they still won't listen, they act as if they like to get their hearts broken. I am concerned with how years pass and nothing seems to ever change.

It was no fan fare when it came down to laying the ladies down, they spreaded it out, eagerly not knowing what was in store.

I tried to caress them and leave nothing, yet the suave kids smile left their soul tossing and turning. I wondered what had gotten into them; I told my boy that these ladies acted like they were "aDickted". Showing up and I showed out in the covers. To me that wasn't love it was just affection, you but it was love to the shortys' they were falling head over hills. How you going to be in love with a brother that you don't even know.

Already head over heals, in love just from vibes and stares, then once we handle that bottom you melt like chocolate and try to stick like honey, finessing your way into brothers heart. We are intricate, meaning complicated motherfuckers. Yes us men. We like a puzzle wit some missing dam pieces. Click, click shall I start moving these big dam pieces, while you study hanging on to me.

I was like a clock for sure back in the day steady moving, couldn't pause for a second or things would not be right. Don't jam up a movement or you might as well throw it out and know that everything is off. We don't value emotion, so you really think we care when you trying to show it. Well sincerely, until we learn as we get older, how to become open hearted individuals. Nothing is ever right. We are not about to look weak or solve problems we know we didn't cause, or even have a clue of fixing correctly. Love is a game that's meant to be played by two. Yet one always wants to leave. Just as many of us run for the same reasons that we stay. Unfamiliarity, struggle, fear and the pattern of not being able to conquer the things we should, this is what makes us dress to a new slate quicker than you can say fire.

Once there was one pouring out her affection, verbally turning me on, yet slaying me all at the same time. I lay with here smiled and had nothing verbally to attach all of my actions were in the physical. So in other words I had her believing everything I told her. I'm sure she told other girls about our magic and she clung to this unspoken, attachment, a damn promise that I had never given her heart. Cheater yes that's what she called me when she saw me with the young lady who spoke no words and was inexperienced and silent, yet I knew she could hold my heart and my words.

I knew, as I loved this woman physically that I would never have to worry about her shedding pieces of my soul to anyone. I lay marks on her heart through me shutting her down sexually. Theses marks can be simmered down yet they would always remain. I can remember those moments not that I didn't feel bad, I just wasn't trying to cling on to them at that moment. Is this how my father felt, what obligated him to run off from my mother, was he being illogical about the entire situation. Did he even go there emotionally in his mind, how could he understand the pain she would go thru or even the discomfort of my soul, having to grow up without him.

My partners weren't perfect role models, I saw so many ladies that they went thru it was like a movie, damn multiple movies. Do you have enough time to listen? I went to a party late one February it was kind of chilly, foxy ladies still had that skin glistening even though it was kind of chalky and cold out. My boy was known for having a little get together and the ladies treated him like he was someone extra special. He had a steady girlfriend Leslie, she had a kid by him, and Leslie wasn't around often. It was a big occasion when she delivered his bundle of joy, yet that excitement was short lived. I wondered where the damn joy went too. You mean to tell me that there is nothing exciting about having a little girl, after time passes.

A lie, the fact is you mean mugging, grumpy as hell now she got a shitty attitude, because she don't understand what you going through emotionally. You can't see the light in a dark tunnel so you just start trying to run on through, banging shit up, like hearts, emotions, mental moods and sometimes physical. Sarah was a sexy chick, she was my partner other girl, the one that got all the attention, she was a whore in more than one-way.

She sold about as much product as me working for some dude that had came through our area, my boy didn't know at first that she even sold weed or anything. Anytime you on the chain gang selling some product, there is always someone above you supplying it's as if you never get to the top of the chain. Depends on who your supplier is that is why it's so hard to get out the game.

Sarah was selling, I just was glad she stayed out of my area; I wouldn't have wanted to have to set her straight. I had to keep my hustle going no matter what. At this particular party, Sarah couldn't keep still, she constantly kept going outside, and my boy couldn't understand why she kept disappearing. By the time Lennox figured out that Sarah must have been outside somewhere he strolled out there somewhat tipsy and walked around a bit. He got back to the porch and was looking like he was fuming. One of the dirty instigators said, "Oh she out here and laughed as he walked inside". Bro turned around and called her name, "Sarah"!!

As homey spun around he must have saw her reflection in a car window down the block. He ran down that way and started cursing, saying all kinds of shit. Some dude jumped out of the driver's side and pulled a glock on my homey; Sarah leaped from the car and begged him not to shoot him. Trigger wasn't pulled and Lennox pulled his dude got in the car and pulled off.

As Sarah and Lennox continued to scream as they came up the block all of a sudden that same car dashed back through and a few shots were fired in the air. Homey talked about that incident a few days and was angry he couldn't figure out who that nigga really was; I was more upset he wouldn't let that trick go. If you cant shake a feeling. Quit the fucking dealing. Instinct is more important than anything basic, at that. Believe it or not God gives us that instinct.

Lennox had some kind of major deal going down, he hadn't spoke to me about it personally so I didn't ask, he must have told ole shady Sarah what he had planned because you wouldn't believe how they set him up. There were many people who worked under Lennox and on a certain date he always went turned the money into the power Lord above him. People say Lennox, was about to leave his place to meet someone, when Sarah popped up trying to convince how much she loved him by apologizing like the freak she was. Just like most young brothers he couldn't turn the nasty naughtiness down. In the midst of getting his pants down she got his wrist into some cuffs he figured she was just being naughty.

A few moments later some busters burst in and took all his loot and beat the hell out of him, within an inch of his life. This right here opened my eyes to how slick some chicks were. I became careful for sure. Could I keep living on the edge like this or would I meet a shifty broad like this with a set up on her mind? I tried to shift gears for a second.

I spent lots of time in the street and I got caught up with the police. I wasn't as wise as I thought I was, I never would've gotten caught if I had of understood more about the game. I was arrested for possession it was nothing to freak me out. I looked at the rest of those brothers like they were enemies and some as acquaintances from the block.

I did what I did and nobody was responsible for my tumble but me. I had watched a whole bunch of dudes get done in. I lay there and looked at the cell only as I came out of dreams did my train of thought shift; I had no problems I was just focusing. Where I could be, where I should be, instead of wasting time there like I was doing sitting behind those bars. I looked at every crevice on the wall and looked at my surroundings, how long would it be before I could be back on the street.

My homeboy that was like a brother to me, taught me so much about street life. Survival just wasn't the thing that was important. We were trying to build dreams together. He was planning on building his magazine to greater heights. His clothing designs were fierce. I watched and he taught me how to keep a dream alive even if it was almost dead. I was taught to never let go of hope as long as I was above ground and could clearly find a way to prosper. Other dudes sat in jail giving up hope, while some plotted what the next territory would be.

(My bestfriend's headstone.)

Clearly the nights I had slept on the streets alone and didn't want to knock on any doors or bother any one else he was right there for me. It was like serving in a camp meant for family. When you grow you must learn to extend yourself no matter the circumstance. I only want to get through each moment, no matter the pain of the trial by learning to adjust to any situation I can be presented in life.

As I did my short bid I was acknowledging, the dudes that had fantastic art finesse, the amazing graphics they could do without any professional learning. I sat and watched them maneuver their skills like they had been taught professionally when they never had been. I saw one dude called "Block" there was not one pattern that he couldn't conjure up, as the men

Lay their getting life etched on their backs, necks or biceps. They were getting history, remnants that would be forever reminders. It's more epic than anyone realizes as you try to paint that ghetto, island art, mystic or comical art on the body. I felt a trigger and I wanted to shoot some ink too. I watched as the other artists played Rembrandt on peoples bodies.

I closely paid attention and I started taking positive ink sessions on brothers. I never had a complaint I did the most expressive and vivid designs anyone had ever seen. I often gave engaging direction on what they should do, when they would give a glimpse on what they wanted to have created on their canvas. I had many heart to heart conversations with fellow brothers and I witnessed the deep sentiments to mothers, the wifey, children or even girlfriends.

A lot of powerful emotions were in each little prickle. Every ounce of ink, every subjected tingle and rivet of the artistic gun I was firing. I ended up using that for many of my many side hustles that I needed to get me some stacks when I was out in the free world. I picked up my drawing game and started designing all types of things for people T-shirts along with subtle graphics for others. My homeboy was happy that I learned how to put use every ounce of workable and technique that I had learned during of my life.

Chapter 6
Girls, Girls, Girls

What happens when you cross somebody's path, something electric goes through you, being showboat oozes out of you, getting to know that person is always open? Vibes hit conquer you like, it's like a light shower not a full storm but you want to be caught up in it no matter the weather. No doubt this fireball wanted to know me also, her eyes had been engaging. I stepped on campus, fresh boots, nice jacket and head bobbing from side to side, listening to some beats. I noticed eyes followed me like shadows on a wall at noon. I went to my first class trying to ignore the beauties that were scoping me, with a quickness they were on a brother like they were planning for the future. I wasn't prepping to be nobody's husband I just wanted to get some skins, when I could.

On the way to a class some home boys caught up with me, and asked had I heard about a dope boy that used to hang with us, "they said he had two chicks knocked up at once". Shit, it was all-amusing to me, I knew fully brother was stressing. We love to act like we big pimping, yet ready for war when the ladies come with their barrage of words. Hostile and full of fire, women don't let up either, they will leave your ass feeling like, they just ran over you with a tanker. People you must learn, you reap what you sow, nothing happens in life without its repercussions.

We glided through the hall when I saw Angie, somebody passed her and called her, "Dreamy" well that's what I was calling her too, and she had me in another constellation for a while. She was cute and had a semi-innocent grin, yeah semi.

Why is it we always want to blame the woman and don't want to take responsibility for anything that we caused? We want to steer clear of emotion and set the tone for the relationship, a lot of times we are unable to set the tone. We aren't thinking responsibly as we try and capture, it's all about the stick and move. If girls only knew how shallow we were thinking, yet mentally we not that tuff, different package with sorted emotions. They need to realize how many lies we could tell, just to convince you to be with us.

Angie and I starting hanging together the sex was bombastic, we were teaching each other how to be joined at the hip because of sex, no other reason. Nothing big did we have in common yet we certainly had an attraction to each other. Her mood swings were there but, so at times I still did my own thing. It's something how you can't understand what love is yet when you learn it's too late for the past, yet just right for the future. Angie and I hadn't made plans about the future or anything, it was just life and we were young. People of course were jealous of our relationship, it had no

(My friend and I in 2012)

appeal to Angie, and little did they know I thought we were inseparable.

It starts to worry a brother, though we will never formally admit it, when a female starts changing her attitude like she changes draws. You want to know how that is, well it's frequently. It all begun to seem a little different when Angie started being very quiet, she wasn't so vocal at all. I wondered why she became slightly distant and didn't even joke like she used too. I assumed it was beef with her parents. Angie and her parents always had their problems with each other.

I consoled her when it was necessary. I noticed, even her appearance went down a notch and she seemed sort of in a shambles. I told Angie lets get together and we did one evening. I had my mind on making things right between us. I wanted to make everything better some through a physical sense; she just wanted to have conversation. You couldn't believe what she opened up to me about.

Angie told me that she was pregnant, dam could this be happening right now. Man, what did I just say, what goes around comes around. I was so busy laughing about other dudes and their problems now I got a situation. Now here I am expecting a child of my own and calling it a situation. We know we would take great offense in having someone talk about a child that we created, yet here we are acting like they all aint shit before they are born.

I quickly snapped into gear, I was determined to give my child a good life. I thought about the missing moments that were in my life because my father was not around. If I could conquer four or five of those moments, I would be a changed man. The open pain and lacerations of the soul that a man can feel, just from the unsolicited pain a woman unleashes on him; you never know what destiny has in store. So harbor no resentment and tell no lies. Understand what you can of someone else's battle cry. Angie had a lot of pain, discomfort and uneasiness those future months. I tried to love her as best that I could at the moment, we had a lot of broken moments where we didn't know how to challenge life in the next game.

Being a parent in High School was going to be hard enough, without any added pressures from, parents, peers, friends or anyone. The pregnancy was so rocky and I ended up grieving, my first son died on April 18th 2005, his name was Omari Markeese Ballard, his mother lost him due to a miscarriage at 7 months. The pain split us in a way we could no survive as a couple. I hoped music would heal me.

Chapter 7
Growing Fast

Age can determine how you learn, and the value of generating new ideas to be able to grow in this world. The most important way a stoic heart can grow is through dire circumstances. Don't get me wrong this isn't some pity party. This is a cognac infused moment; my moment is aromatic, serious and charged. I have never wanted to grow up without missing anything. I feel the need to get a full view of life; I don't want a partial eclipse then end up just howling at the moon. I will bark but I choose to never bite.

Looking back on my busy road play, I've been thinking about how I got the travel bug honestly. Mom was a soldier and she was always on the move. We constantly traveled over the country military base to military base; there are so many beautiful, scenes in this country to appreciate. We often made friends that we could never forget, yet they stayed so deep in hearts we felt they tugged with anchors. Were we ever satisfied with our way of living did we know this to be living. I can remember back when I was super young I smiled at the female soldiers with the largest smiles, looking from the legs, to the uniform, to the smile, to the uniform, to the hair and back down to the uniform. I only wanted to keep smiling and perhaps get to know as many new people as possible.

Mom was sent to a base in San Diego, where the sunshine was magnificent and the aroma was exhilarating. Cool men tried to dictate the scene and most of the women par took in someone's dreams.

Mom's smile seemed to become grateful and overflowing, I payed attention to her visitors. I wondered how our night would turn different. Would new friends be embedded in our memory? The memories in San Diego I didn't want to let go of.

Mom had a really good friend that she enjoyed hanging with while we lived in San Diego her name was Mary. Mary's was married to Super Producer Dr. Dre's brother. Her son Marvin and I went to school together we had quite a bit in common and loved to play after school. We would hang together jumping around dancing and rapping, singing hits we heard on the radio. People noticed us, and Mary's husband wanted us to come to the studio sing and rap a little. We were sounding so good and our flow was so straight that people couldn't even keep their eyes off of us. People started calling us the new Chris Cross.

I remember sitting watching cartoons and waiting for mom to finished getting dressed. I would do my little steps and laugh. It was all excitement to me, one Saturday as mom was in her mirror getting ready for a nice afternoon, with friends I stood up between cartoon commercials dancing and playing around. It was all fun to me, I didn't realize how amazing it was to everyone else that we could get down so. Hmm, I loved to rock out even as a youngster didn't know how I would love music later in life and be reintroduced. I was just a small kid and every thing about this made me smile. Mom was laughing at me and the little moves I was making. She thought her little boy was too cute as he did steps and tried to act like he was on someone's stage. We left home and mom dropped me off with my friend so that we could have our unique play date.

Boom boom boom ba da ba da, pop bad a bad a Boom. It was resonating out the building, and it was hitting the air with great enthusiasm. I strolled in there age 5, yet seemed like I was going on 50. I truly locked eyes and looked at every single piece of foam, on the walls that determined how the sound resonated through the area. I looked at the plaques and pictures and the vibe made me feel like I had been lifted someplace special. My buddy and I were laughing and tickled we were spitting our raps and doing our dances showing people the magic we could make. I looked at the control board not having a clue as to how far it could take us. I truly believed in the magic we were making. The good time we had has truly been a stepping-stone to future corners I would cross.

Everywhere I went people started to call us the new Chris Cross, we got the attention of many producers in the area that were hanging with. I remember us hanging out at the studio and listening back at our vocals being replayed. It was the most awesome feeling ever. Shoot, it hadn't occurred to me that this was more than fun, and that coincidently in the future when I became an adult I would still want to push so much of my heart and soul out into many verses. How significant it is that all the small moldings of a child helped him become a man. The tears and sniffles, from a young man because of scrapes and bump help him learn resilience. Down to the fanfare and small accolades we gather as we are learn from teamwork, patience and kindness.

We performed and entertained for many people. Our mothers were extremely good friends, they were very proud of their young men. Mom loved that weather out there in San Diego and I didn't know that place on the map from anywhere else. I would grow to understand the beauty of travel and the appreciation of profound people and great cities. New places and faces were on the horizon again, I didn't know why we had to leave but, I knew it was going to be a sad day to not be able to hang out not just performing, but playing too.

I would have dreams about a dark stage, lights flashing as a little guy wondering into the middle stage and morphing into a man. I would always see myself reaching trying to touch so many people. I wanted to help them. In my dream on lookers would outstretch their hand and as I reached them almost, the stage would rise and rise. Weird dreams like that never really bothered me, but every moment where I felt I learned something new to my survival, was more than grand. I wanted to apply all I could to life in the future I knew that would help become the man I wanted to be.

Years passed, I exported music to the back of my mind, don't get me wrong, I loved it I just wasn't about to take it on as a career. It would be years later when I discovered music was my love again. I spent junior high and teen years, playing basketball, running track and playing baseball. Life is just like sports a game. I know when you hear that, you probably think of that in a negative context. It doesn't have to be.

You have the questions, the answers you should seek and there are different plays that need to be made in order to succeed in whatever game. I never was one to be outspoken or a bully. I wanted to build upon whatever foundation I had. Sometimes I assumed foundations that know one else could notice. I would be able to see a molehill and make it out of a mountain. I figured the biggest hill would help me get where I needed to be quicker, fuck taking short cuts. I need to jump out of the airplane and land on the bulls eye. We can never conceive that sliding into home or, stealing a base or even striking out and never making it home will get you just what you need.

I remember watching my coach talk to the other players, I said to myself dam, he talk too much. I thought to myself that there was no possible way that I was going to go thru all of the combinations he suggested. I figured, I wouldn't need to learn all of that or know all of that. There is always more to the system than a man expects so always be prepared. I remember at practice the coach had so many complaints. What could I do to get him to drop some of the rhetoric and just let us swing the bat? I didn't feel like being in the middle of a sermon every time I went to practice.

My stance wasn't good enough they said, so I was asked to step to the side. My coach said "my body language would get me in trouble" what the heck did he mean by that? All of a sudden I was out there running around the field. Coach had us doing conditioning with medicine balls, running round looking like we had lost our mind. I did so man crazy lunges and leg stretches I thought I could step up a hill. I was learning that there is prep for all things. No matter how I disliked it, I had to adjust to it all.

All of the vertical lifts that my body held up for, each day after time made me better. Discipline hadn't been my strongest suit yet I learned why preparation was so important. I would grow to not fight against people who were teaching me. I gained a lot of piece from being out on the field at batting practice. It was almost like I was knocking my problems to the sky.

Chapter 8
Dreams

I was running as fast as I could the sound of another pair of foot prints pushing just as hard next to mine. Concrete getting slapped so hard it seemed as if dents were being pounded into the pavement. Where there were puddles of oil and water they slammed upward from the pounding of our feet and bolted toward the sky splattering the Heavens. The night was so ridiculously black, all of my effort went into trying to imagine, the way home instead of seeing it clearly. God was letting his angel's presence be known, all of a sudden it seemed as if I was flying, not just body moving fast, but I was above it all.

I watched as the silver bullets whizzed by and I saw one of my homeboys, jerk forward, he stammered slowly but didn't fall. The corner was embraced as quickly as he ran. I thought he had grown wings, as he jetted across a street into an alleyway. I lost sight of him, I only saw a gray fog and a sparkling flicker as I coasted above all, that was important to me was below.

Some booming bass and thumping beats rolled off of the radio as I woke up in a hot sweat. My head was pulsating, dam; you jus don't even understand how I felt. This was this same dream that had been occurring to me over and over again. Several of my homeboys had been shot lately and my dreams were convincing me that it was going to happen again. There were places I didn't like to revisit, places from my dreams where I had lost friends.

Street life is not for the weak at heart; so don't go crying any tears. I got up and put my Timbs on and Military jacket. I was trying to be ready for anything, now would I be is the question, its hard to even say.

My tongue was always slick, I had a way of saying things that could easily have people cracking up. Folks said I had a versatile flow. I wasn't going to let my life be always about the hard times. I wanted my life to be about the end result of a hustle. I always let the music been apart of what motivated me it dug deeper into my soul more than I can explain. I used to rap the flows of the best, yet I was always digging deep into myself, when you reach into your soul a way can be created for anything I had a partner that knew he was deep on the music kick.

My brother from another mother Chris knew so much about music and studios shit, I thought he was going to be on some magazine covers real soon. Hell he was running a magazine himself, I'm following into his footsteps. Chris designed clothes and knew every entrepreneurial flow there was. I wanted to be just like him, he was the boss for sure. He was heavy into the dope game. I kept my flow to a minimum. My brother was trying to get on another level.

I was introduced to a chick named Crystal at my brother's house she invited me to this little club aka a "Hole in the wall" called "Beamer's" that she frequented. I told her that I would be through later that afternoon I had a couple more blocks to turn. I went with my bro to pick up a package he did all the talking, he had told me to watch how this Negro was going to try and play him. Sure enough some words were exchanged and dude got mad, my bro knew he was trying to hustle him. Had product that looked like some basil and other herbs rather than the real deal that was supposed to be smoked. Goons didn't look like they were locked and loaded, yet my brother showed me how to be prepared incase they wanted to act a fool.

The deal didn't go thru; we left with our pockets still full, no new product but also with our lives. I could not ask for more than that I was not ready for my epitaph to be on any tombstone. Hell it's quite normal at times to be a broke dope boy. Chris wasn't having that, he never slept, and his time was spent thinking of another extreme master plan. He was closer than blood, when I say brother know that I am talking about Chris, he took me under his wing like I hadn't expected anyone to do at all.

My bro didn't think that hustling was sensible at all he wanted to make sure he kept extra loot. He never wanted to be just some broke figga from our hood, fronting like he had something that he knew he didn't.

I had so many brothers who were looking out for me, trying to teach me all levels to this life. I never expected I would lose any of them so soon. I asked my Bro about Crystal he explained that she would bring a lot of excitement to my life; hey I was down for that. My Bro said she was a dancer and a waitress at the Club, Beamers. I was thinking to myself. Damn, I want to possibly see her in action. Word was that Crystal, a few other sexy acquaintances could sing and freestyle, so they also used to hang out at the studio he was taking me too.

My excitement level went to another level as we entered the building. We were at a recording studio. As we turned the corners inside I could here a minor thump that pulsated my heart and it was making love to the floors as it made love to my senses. There were some cats there spitting bars as we walked in, you could tell they had been committed to the dedication on this grind. You could tell these boys were full of ambition.

I got along with everyone, it was like a family whom I met up with and hadn't seen in forever. The feeling was electric, like some rapper often says. Was Ben Franklin here in person, to live out the best moment of life because they had it going on up in there. My

(My brother and I. Doing the damn thing!)

people, music was playing back and it sounded like the delivery was more than federal express it was, here with an authority that could not be explained.

We were amped up some full of liquor others blowing smoke ahh the element was powerful and the mood was righteous. A few hotties trickled in and talked to various sources there. I just spoke up on how wonderful it was that the tracks had such fire. They sounded bold and full of the truths of our hood. My brother Laughed, and told me, "You can do It". Naw, not me, this is something I wanted to do at home just jamming to the music, I never thought of blazing tracks like this. We sat down and my Bro started to show me how to write raps, how to become one with the music and it was like I was born for it.

My life seemed like it could change before my eyes. My brother/ best friend Chris booked a session for me, I dropped a few bars and I couldn't even stop tripping. Dam I was sounding so good. I couldn't believe it. My brother was proud of me and the strides I was making, we started a group together called Circuit. Now let me tell you we were about to blow something up. This was going to take us in another direction; we had to be on our way to a more positive space than we had been.

I got so caught up in the studio time and how we had been blazing those tracks that it was forever before I made it to Beamers. Late that night I had that same dream about running. These night sweats was about to drown me and I was going to turn so violent in my bed that I was about to hurt myself. How can we get so deep within ourselves that dreams scream every bit of reality? I tried to shake every ounce of the vibe; I headed to the studio and recorded with my boy we had that game crushing hits popping. I learned so much about life about life, from my brother and others. There is always one to want to cut you down just as you stand up. Life is never flawless expect it all. Absolutely nothing in life is going to short change just because it's headed in your direction. After all, don't you know it increases speed?

When I stepped into Beamers, music would be a ten and eyes would be hitting me with hard glances coming from every direction. I would have other girls tingling to sample this candy store. I would run up to Beamers and do my best to connect with Crystal. I was being hypnotized as I walked in the door. Power can come in many packages you just never know what your destiny is going to lead you to. Crystal was my sweet spot at the moment; she knew how to push every button I had and stroke every bit of me. I remember once she called me to the rest room and um wanted to punish me for being late as I came through to see her. Although just as quick as I was punished, I was rewarded. Her lips were powerful and succulent. I mistakenly bit one once, there is no need to be shamed. Se tasted like paradise if it could b a set of lips.

Crystal always would tell me all of her secrets. I kept quiet about them to my homeboys, knowing I didn't need to focus on too much stuff. My baby being as gorgeous as she was, got plenty of action started. I never confused her business with pleasure; it's a big enough problem to confuse so I kept cool all the time. One night I got a call from Hammer a partner of ours who was running drugs through some different areas. He asked where my Bro was and told him I wasn't sure. Normally if someone called to check on one of us, we would, pick up the phone and holla at the other one to let them know that were on the radar (being looked for), I was being lazy this day so I didn't hit him up. I was hanging out with Crystal more than I was slanging product. I practically had given it up. I had fallen in love with another girl, Music the vibe had me by the jugular, and I stayed in the studio constantly you couldn't get me to leave for anything.

My Brother always seemed to keep up with the hustle in the street even though we many other things going on. For a minute we kind of didn't see each other though we were street family it was like we were blood brothers our bond was just as strong. I was laying up with Crystal when I started having these funny feelings in my stomach and chest, I became so dam uncomfortable that I tried my best to go to sleep and hoped that would make it disappear.

Yet it started again I was running, running, dodging bullets, feet slamming so hard on the concrete as I was putting it down that I was about to break the concrete. The little mist of water that was on the ground slammed up ward I was running for my life and I could look over and see my brother was running for his with me. I was getting so dam sick of these dreams I didn't know what to do. They were agitating me so much, that I was becoming a little bitter toward my girl.

Someone called asking about my boy for the second day in a row. Now this made me suspicious, I called to see was he okay, he said, "Sure I am, just make sure you stay careful in them streets". Yes, he did the random preaching. He was worried about me and what I would get into. I went and turned a few blocks this day and the clouds looked darker than they had been. You know how you can smell the rain, I could tell sooner rather than later it would be coming down. I ran into one of our partners he asked could I make a run later and, I said I would holler back at him.

As I walked back home I had my music banging in my ear, I was impressed at our music even if I did have to say so myself. Soon hell we could be blowing up their charts and really give these knuckleheads something to talk about. I turned the corner about a block away from Crystals place a car kind of pulled up on me, kind of slanted like cutting me off and I'm trying to cross the street.

This random brother and me locked eyes before he could reach for anything, I ran then cut across the street and down the block. I went past Crystal's house because I didn't want anyone following me there. Now I was wondering what the hell was going down. I got away then called my boy named Spook and told him what happened. I couldn't reach my Brother; I was in a reckless mood. I thought about the run I was supposed to make and decided not too. I made it over to Crystals and I was frustrated, I didn't think this would be so crazy. I really didn't want her out of my eyesight that night. People had shot so many people in the neighborhood. It was a war zone. Now was that incident random or was it planned. Crystal insisted on going down to the bar they said they needed her to work.

Crystal went into work about 6 that evening I decided I would head down there to surprise her. No need to hide from anything if there is a reason, forget about it, what ever is meant to get you will. I strolled in, sat down looked around and happen to see a dude I knew. As Rome came over and began a conversation he told me my brother was supposed to be meeting someone about a deal gone bad, yet he knew no names. My brother had tried to get a little something straight; he was coming through any minute now.

Almost simultaneously I looked up and the dude was there in my view. Chris was very wild-eyed, high even it seemed. He told me not to misuse the product and he got caught up in the mix. These renegades weren't anyone to play with. I only hoped he could handle things the correct way. I asked, "Was there anything I could do for him?" He said "no". We went to a corner booth n he shifted money around that he had gotten from someone.

My brother was getting counterfeit money and trying to replace what he hadn't made. He was trying to replace what a demon had defiled; the demon had caused him to become another soul lost within a habit. We all watched as this young man immersed himself into a contagious product that had destroyed the best futures, the greatest hopes and the most profound dreams. We all would be mad that this couldn't be traced to just some demon; it was like episodes of vanish. How could your habit become your problem, so easy it does become it? It's the greatest souls who may be going through their own struggles and wars yet they cheer for us. I watched as my brother left he seemed to fade out of my eyesight. I almost felt a pain, I got really weak as I saw my brother vanish then I got up and ran out of the door, it was misting rain.

I was running as fast as I could the sound of another pair of foot prints seemed to be pushing just as hard next to mine. Concrete getting slapped so hard it seemed as if dents were being pounded into the pavement. Where there were puddles of oil and water they slammed upward from the pounding of our feet and bolted toward the sky splattering the Heavens. The night was so ridiculously black, all of my effort went into trying to imagine, the way to safety.

Instead of seeing the way clearly God was letting his angel's presence be known, all of a sudden it seemed as if I was flying, my feet didn't seem to be touching the ground. I suddenly looked back almost as if I had given up and nobody was there. I guess the same guys whom I assumed were chasing me were running behind someone else.

It was almost as if I didn't exist for a minute, and was invisible. I turned the corner and didn't breathe for a second, I held my body so still and wasn't even able to exhale at all. I heard some voices and didn't want to know at all who it might be. I wondered where Rome was, yet he wasn't the type to go for bad, he is more so the type to leave you hanging. As I kept up the block I saw sparks flying as I turned the corner. I saw the Shadow of Chris hit the ground. I froze intently and never looked around the corner but heard cars screeching off. I heard other random shots and ran as fast as I possibly could. I didn't want to confirm that It was exactly whom I envisioned. I felt as if I had just loss my breath. Winded I ran and ran never looking back.

I crept back toward Crystals work place I was staggering breathing hard did I see what I saw, Rome was standing talking to a guard he had a wound in his shoulder. I didn't try to find out how he got wounded, I just eased back into the building. I saw Crystal talking to one of the other girls looking confused and frantic. I looked down and realized my phone was blinking, dam they were looking for me. I had the jitters so I didn't answer the phone. No more dream like moments coming to life or would tonight be the end for me also.

The fellas were calling me, I didn't want to see had they heard the news my best friend/ my brother Chris had been gunned down round, would this be the confirmation. I suddenly got the news that my best friend/my brother had been murdered over a drug deal gone wrong. Damn, how the hell did this happen, you lose a part of you when you lose someone that's that close to you. I was so hurt period. I didn't sleep for days, for weeks, when I finally did that dream remained. His ghost constantly haunted me terribly for those first years for various reasons. I would see him, I would see the ghost walking through the house and I would just break out into sweats. Even as I reminisce now it still happens from time to time

Chapter 9
For The Wrong Reason

One Saturday night I found myself riding "shotgun" next to my father. Things weren't going to well for me back in Atlanta, so my mother suggested that I comeback there to get up on my feet. It was appealing and crazy, because I knew the road of change was ahead of me. You can try to build up though you are already down in a tunnel, within a private war zone. The whole ride there was rather awkward. Hell, what was I going to say?

Is what I was thinking to my self, because I was sitting next to a man I didn't really know. Do I count how many birds in the sky or watch and see how much the clouds move, as we travel? I couldn't let my pride destroy the next part of my journey. While sitting there I thought about my next moves in this segment of my life.

The thought about kind of moving back in with my mom was over the top. This means curfews and someone putting tabs on your every move. Is it just instinct or do mothers not understand that we can make it work without a protector. No more freedom! Would I be able to get thru this turmoil and slight agitation, Some times the people that mean well can cost the most pain. When we reached our destination, she was parked sitting in her car to the left of us. After we said our fair wells and good byes, I transitioned into mom's car. I didn't even want to begin thinking about the road ahead.

It was weird seeing them actually talk to each other; the stance they had made in life had nothing to do with what I wanted or me. The relationship they conjured up merely was based on what they thought it should be after their disagreements. All I could do was ride with it and not cause any problems. I was drained feeling down and mind going all over, I just wanted some peace, and I knew it wouldn't be potentially hard to focus on the things at hand. While my mother was preaching about the laws of the house, my mind was elsewhere. I wasn't paying her any attention.

As the raindrops created a rhythm against the windshield, I clearly saw highlights of my life playing back in chronological order. I wasn't too pleased with my decision and where I currently stood in my life. Don't get me wrong. I could've been dead so many times; it was a blessing to get another opportunity to start fresh. I had run into so many close calls and knew that I should be starting over. I didn't want to ask anyone for anything or have to rely on others though I knew it was important that I take responsibility for the correct things. Looking for a job was first on my to do list.

When we reached my mothers house, she showed me to my room. As I laid across the bed, in this dark room, the sound of rain falling instantly put me to sleep. The following morning I woke up to the loud projections of my mother's voice. "DJ, get up now!" was the hook to the soundtrack that morning. It kind of reminded me how she used to wake me up, years back. All I could do was shake my head. Later on that morning, she dropped me off at the community college not to far from her job.

I ended up going to the campus library, to fill some job applications. I walked around and noticed it was a busy day saw a few old faces that I remember from the past and a few that I wanted to keep it that way. In the midst of doing that, I noticed one of my homeboys sitting a few rows down. He and I chopped it up for a few, until I seen this beautiful young lady walking towards the printing station. It seemed as if the entire library came to an immediate silence.

Eyes rotated, lips curved and glistened, throats gulped. My friend and I debated back and forth on who was going to talk to her. Well, that was short lived; I just got up to approach her. The initial approach was unusual because, the conversation flooded so well. We conversed for damn near two hours. Before she left I asked for her phone number, but was rejected. The young lady did request mine although.

I was thinking to myself. Shorty spent all this time having a convo with me, when she didn't even care to give me the number.

Wow, how was she going to shut me down like that? Fellas, I'm sure you can feel me on this one. This situation was on some bullshit for real. Didn't have the time, so definitely I wasn't about to lose any sleep over that kind of crap.

Relationships should either come or go, never take em so serious that you need to lose any moments of peace. You win some; you lose some that's how you play the game. A few days past and I hadn't even thought of the young lady from the school. My mother and I happened to walk in the front door. Suddenly I started to feel my phone vibrating in my pocket. I took it out my pocket and to my surprise; the chick from the library had sent me a text message. Now you all know I had a huge cool aid smile on my face.

That hot conversation, needed up with her pulling up in front of my mothers house, later on that evening. I looked out of the window and walked to the mirror and brushed myself off before I walked out. I tried not to move too fast, nor. It was an anxious moment for this cool cat. As I walked toward her car, I smiled to myself. I was instantly amused that this twenty-one year old was riding clean as hell. She was looking astonishing as well. In my head I was like, "Oh shit I got a winner". Starting that night we continued to kick it kind of hard.

I really enjoyed her company. Even though I was really attracted to her physically, she was really a cool individual. We shared so many things in common. As many curves as she had on her body they kept me dazed and confused. I was steadily building upon her mountain, trying to climb her tower instead of trying to the things I needed to do.

I was focusing on the minute, her strands of hair, and her reflected colors that appear within her eyes. The stamina of physical things is more important in the beginning than they are at the end. Lips are filled with lies that we call truths at the opening of our hearts. Yet as there is a closing and things begin to dwindle we notice all of the things we should have noticed before. I felt true to her.

While spending a lot of time with her I was losing focus on my priorities. My mother was giving me some turbulence about it. She even went as far as telling my girlfriend I wasn't worth her time. Then gave her the spell on how my father did her, as if it was some kind resemblance. Luckily that didn't alter her decisions to be with me. After that ordeal and dealing with the balance beam between her and my mother. I picked up several odd jobs and enrolled back into college. I would've never known that a woman has the power to influence a man to do just about anything. I know one thing Shorty had my head gone for real.

To be honest I felt good about myself and life was grand. Everything I was doing was legit and my agenda was falling into place. We had had some sexy times; there was no clue that tides were changing. One Friday morning I was in class staring out of the window. It wasn't too long before I saw my girl's car pull up on the parking lot. It was kind of weird because she was a few hours early and I'd noticed that she had called me several times. Back to back calls like that something had to desperately be wrong. I gathered my things, signed out and raced out of the doo and out of the building.

Before I entered her car I knew it was some shit. Something just didn't seem right. I felt the weirdest feeling. As I looked at her intently she had a nervous look on her face. Before I could say a world she said, "Look at what the doctor gave me". After she said those words she dropped a bag in my lap. The bag had several parenting books inside. Was I shocked? Yes it was a shocking surprise! Not with all the sexual activity we had been having some would say. I didn't expect it. Once she gave me the news it became extremely quiet. All you could hear was heartbeats and heavy raindrops. The atmosphere had spun and did a 360 just that quickly.

That conversation ended differently than I expected. All I knew is that we weren't considering abortions. From that point on, things desperately changed. I was going to see a side of her that I didn't want to encounter. Here is when everything began to take such an awkward and uncomfortable turn. Right after she told me about us expecting a child, I withdrew from school. How could I focus on school when I needed to prepare for the future, I knew if I were to work it would be difficult to study for school. All I could think about was not making the same mistakes my father made. We had so many ups and downs yet I was still trying to hang in there and be there for her. But of course because I was the male I was constantly given all of the blame.

I proposed to her because I wanted my son to come home to a complete home situation. Things really started to take an opposite turn when other people were intent on getting involved. My mother was admitting about throwing her salt in the situation. It was also hard because her mother wanted to spin everything in a negative way. She already wasn't too fond of me because I was black. My son was so handsome. He was my reason for waking up. I constantly held him. His smile could light all of Paris and a million other cities also. When he was born was the proudest moment ever. I wanted to be an example for him, yet it was hard to do things the right way.

Just by being in Atlanta dam, it had me back in my old environment. That was enough to create a lot of confusion. I had not always been a role model. Mind you, I'm proud to say that I never cheated on her, but the world's influence caused us to have more problems than we could possibly bare as a couple. We agreed to just separate awhile. Her and my son agreed to go to Ohio to live with some of her relatives. This was supposed to be a temporary situation. I guess she decided she wanted to separate and make this permanent soon after. There is no telling who was whispering in her ear and influencing her.

A divorce summons was delivered to me a month later.
Talking about being torn to pieces, I can't even explain, how heartbroken I was. I was torn entirely to pieces. A woman that exchanged vows with me left me out to dry. Dam how the hell could this even happen? I thought we were in love and just going through a trial. Dam I know the vows said, "For better of for worse", but this was not on the memo at all.

She may not agree with this excerpt, but I couldn't put it any other way. The significance of this relationship was me owning up to the" man up" logic. I probably wasn't successful but I have gained a lot of substance and maturity. Ladies I'm not a saint nor was a nigga perfect. I know where my faults lie.

The moral of the story is that I was engaged in a life long commitment for all of the wrong reasons. One of my faults was that I used my son as a pawn in our relationship.

"Example of a Man"

I'm a man of morals and old tradition. My soul is light years beyond my age. I find "Mahogany" quite entertaining. "Just to Satisfy You" is therapeutic to life. Don't judge me because I say "yes mam" and hold open doors until the very last woman enters.

I believe in wearing my finest threads on a daily basis my wavy hair would grasp your attention instantly. Many would say I'm a man of precise distinction. The ladies usually want to faint, once they get a preview of my mannerisms they realize it's rare and were manufactured with pride.

Being consistent shall make you relevant. Until you reach that point you are aiming for. Feast your eyes on exactly what you are trying to be. Take notes and pay homage to a real go-getter.

Chapter 10
Tempos, Beats & Creativity

I was into so many things, trying to get that hustle going, but I vowed to make life straight, for the life of my son. Seeing death and passing through so many drug-infested areas had been deep in my past. I would never ignite it in my future. I found myself feeling super creative. I had a camera that I shelled out plenty for. I kept it with me at all times so that I could take amazing photos of my son. When he was no longer near me, I felt lonely except for when I was looking at those photos. I had to figure out how to survive, I found a new creative spell, and music had been important to me then slowly was my lifesaver.

My best friend Ron "Future" Brown took me to this little studio called the Music Box. It was a fly experience. Ron recorded a record and he got me a session as well. It was a boss experience. Shoot I had nothing written down to spit; it was so many lyrics running through my head. I free styled the entire tracks, I was nervous as hell. I was shooting stuff of the dome with fierce veracity. It was a memorable day. I was nervous but ready to deliver. I did extremely well though. I got a gig doing graphic design as an intern for Terry Miles and Scholonda. I met Master P. through his head of A&R Terry Miles.

I landed a few graphics jobs for Master P also. I always kept graphics as something I could fall back on. Every since the few incarceration days I had in the past where I spent a lot of time

(I had a way with the crowd. This is were I felt at peace.)

drawing and etching. I was homeless at the time when I landed these design jobs. Life was tuff but it wasn't completely over. I used to sleep in the office at night. I thought it was cool of them to allow me to do that. I was learning every inch of the way soaking up all I could mentally.

    I used to sneak in the kitchen they shared with other offices on that floor to steal a bite or two from the fridge at night. I didn't stay in that situation long because I didn't like the fact I was an intern and wasn't getting paid. I truly learned a different type of hustling from those people. Yet the experiences weren't the best, I respect them fully until this day.

My ex girlfriend from college introduced me to Kenyon George. He was working with some well-known producers in Virginia. I let him hear my demo and he signed me to VMC. It was a yearlong contract. We recorded a four-track demo in Teddy's Riley's Studio (Future Studios in Virginia Beach, Va.) once we completed the project we drove down to Atlanta to let Teddy hear the tracks. He enjoyed it and wanted me to be on his "ADDIAS" compilation with a list of other artist. I was hyped up and feeling grand just knowing the best was about to certainly come.

One night his studio mysteriously burnt down and my situation with VMC and Teddy Riley dissolved. When I got back to recording I was a beast, I was on a mission to be the man of music I always was meant to be. I completed my first studio album It was entitled "Ray Ban Music" I was happy as hell once I completed it. I was proud because I finished it and everyone was happy for me. I recorded the whole project in 5 days. My evolution and new lifestyle influenced the whole album. It released June 14, 2010. I been spitting on the mike every since. Dropping gems ever so often so that my fire can light people.

I must confess during the many nights, as I was sleeping under desks, and didn't have any bread to eat. I was figuring out how to make some bread so I could stuff my pockets.

Chapter 11
Flip a Coin

My son was my greatest inspiration; I took umpteenth photos of him. He was a handsome guy just like his father. I was determined to just let him make the world smile like he made me smile. Since I had this amazing camera, I tried to get side work from others by taking photos of birthday parties, weddings and even graduations. I made myself available for who ever needed me. I began to go to the mall and I ran into my homey Dinero, he was good people, kind of crazy like me with a great enterprising mind.

Dinero got me a job in the mall and he showed me some of the best ways to shoot. I already had a deep passion for trying to be a photographer then I went right ahead and started shooting to kill. Who knew I would become the best in the game. Who knew I would be capturing every sexy woman's pose possible behind the eye of my lenses.

One night when I was cold and hungry I took a few pieces of paper off of the desk I was sleeping under and I began to design my magazine cover to cover, articles and all. I thought about my homeboy's dreams and the wishes I had. I thought of how many of my friends had been killed and I wanted to live to see my dreams. Could I go around this country and get some of the most interesting people to interview for my magazine and possibly could I find the sexist women in America model for my Magazine.

My dreams began then. All of the dimes as people call them and have them in a sexy seductive manner exposed themselves. It's easy to see ladies just randomly in bathing suits having curves popping out at you from every angle. I wanted to make this as classy as possible. If you are going to pick a hustle you must pick something that you love. Not only do I love talking to beautiful people and interviewing them I also truly love to take pictures. This love affair with my camera is quite something. I love to keep my finger on the pulse of things.

I founded iDYMES Magazine in 2012 while interning for Hood Starzz Networks/Nolimit Forreal Operated by: Terry Miles and Master P. this amazing gift that I gave myself has allowed me to touch people in 175 countries and my line of work has allowed me to travel to Houston, Miami, Seattle, New York, Newark, Augusta, DC, Dayton Kansas City, New Orleans, San Francisco, Los Angeles, Chicago & Virginia Beach and so many other places. The traveling and the experiences truly are captivating.

My first issue of iDYMES had articles about FloRida, Meek Mill, the beautiful Model Stranje Marie was on the cover and I covered things about the Kreative Orkrestra group. My vision has always been to display beautiful women with class. I was beside myself when I reached out to Shawty Lo's manager Johnny and Tomiko Hope they were excellent people and made sure I got and interview with Shawty Lo. I've had some interviews that are unforgettable. Not to mention the episodes that I needed to shut down from the over hype models who thought they could get into a situation with a young C.E.O. Time and time again I had to explain to the ladies I wasn't available and even if I happen to be available I still wouldn't just let them have their way with me,

A young businessman always notices that people want to make situations bigger than they are. One evening in particular I was in a studio doing a shoot with a model, she made several advances at me, of course she was sexy but how could she possibly act like trying to bone me was more important than the photo shoot that we had to put down. I'm just going to call her "Gem" that is not her name. She pulled out several bikinis and showed me. Gem wanted to know did I desire some nude shots.

I explained that that wasn't important. Almost immediately after shooting the different shots, Gem, seductively jumped on me and wrapped her legs around me, I was like stop, stop and she was grabbing me around my neck licking it in long strokes I suddenly became excited and she became tickled an noticed.. Noooo I exclaimed, I want you all to understand that the mental totally has nothing to do with the physical.

Many ladies don't understand that trying to sleep with a C.E.O. will not boost their stock any more. The earning potential will not go up the ladder any more what so ever, because they want to be with a baller. I like them but I don't say anything if they want to take a small drink to relax before being camera ready. I always keep things appropriate. I see beautiful people all the time I am not going to lose my train of thought because of inches of skin are exposed right in front of me.

I could be any man that I want to be. I choose to be one that is really respectable and one that is going to teach his son how to be respectable an innovator and a champion when it comes to being on top of the game. I don't find my work unappealing. Snakes try and inch their way into your life; they never want you not to be happy. They want you on your belly because someone's been hissing and trying to spill untruths about you. Magazines and social media, websites fabricate, as many things as possible about young people, so that you can have horrible names in the public eye. I can't possibly tell you how such an awkward feeling it is when you must deny rumors, to family or perhaps a girlfriend even. One rumor they derived was that I was dating "Portia Beamon" from Bad girls club Have you perhaps wanted to have correspondence to take place for future work and it is suddenly awkward.

Life can be whatever you make it; one must stay in a moment and make it better. Enjoy every step of the moment and don't disregard the signs that the heavens show you. Gravitate towards things you know that you must build upon. Don't dare hide your heart smile and share your wishes. Its good to grow even when nobody wants you toe be feed. Your tears will handle the watering your heart needs.

Chapter 11.1
Third Eye-Just Blind

I realize that this world holds far more secrets than we care to think about. This world holds far more secrets than we care to expose. Often times we are at battle with the powers that be. The very things we often ask for are the same things that are floating in front of our face, yet we pretend we don't see them.

We can't look at the next person and try and pretend we are unaware of the magic that's held for each of us. Whether there are six Degrees of separation, or whatever you notice. Something is there waiting to help you soar through life.

Yes Jimmy Gates of Silk is my cousin, Florence Ballard of the Supremes was granddad's sister, I was born on the same day as Albert Einstein and I was born at the same Hospital as President Barak Obama. Hmm seems unimportant. Well when we are born we have been given traces of the galaxy within us. You either continue to follow life's correct pattern leaving your imprint from the stars where you gaze or you just happen to ignore every sign that's meant for you to flourish in greatness.

I could have stayed on the path that was filled with destruction and envy. I realized I wanted more and I was going to continue until I succeed. Greatness comes when you do your half. Its not about who gives it to you it's about when you realize the consequences of your actions. Taking from others and pushing bad seeds to grow even worse are not the things that will save you.

Learn to have some power inside. Learn to resist things that aren't meant for. Every cookie on display isn't meant to be eaten. There is a positive force just like there is a negative one. Incase nobody told you some negative things feel good. But all things don't last. If you want hope, happiness, strength and continued blessings you got to work until you have complete and utter understanding.

We want to get mad when things don't go our way. We want to hold our head down when prayers aren't answered; well we ask for the best things possible and then aren't satisfied when the universe grants our plea.

I can remember being bitter about love. Matter of fact I hated love and all it stood for I dared anyone to try and tell me anything. I didn't ever give 100 percent and I would give up to quickly. I would slide across the surface and skim just a little off. You know how we do; we didn't ever want the heart of the matter we would rather pretend we couldn't get too deep. I found that I was the cause of my own suffering. While we run round here screaming," love aint Shit". Shoot love is everything can we just learn to dam acknowledge it in the proper perspective.

Everything is universal; it's of the universe we are broken from a piece of the universe. Sometimes your dreams are so deep and vivid because that really was a reality. The fake stuff is what we make up everyday. I wonder do you want better. I always wanted better. I didn't want to continue waddling through the gutter, hiding from bad guys and dodging bullets. I saw to many friends and comrades fall. I wondered frequently why, was I still here.

You can get all the information you want about this world without even asking and you can get the acclaim you need without speaking or even saying a word. Silence is more golden than you realize. My greatest vision came when I was hungry and sleeping under a desk. You have to look at every person in your life and wonder what are they there to teach you. Stop thinking everyone is meant to hold on to. They are not. We stop our own growth by holding on to people and things that weigh us down

You will often meet people who don't understand or value life, so quit being the plane in the holding pattern. You eventually will circle until you run out of gas. Crashing is not an option. You can be blind cripple and crazy, the third eyes cognition can take you all around this world without moving a muscle. Stop thinking so limited and open your mind. You have everything you need already so use it.

June Garcia
(Derrick Ballard)

Chapter 12
Unconditionally Yours

In 2013, I came back to Virginia, to visit my mother. Really, I came to surprise her for her twentieth year anniversary vowel renewal. Our relationship, haven't been ideal. I wanted to make amends with her and my stepfather. The ceremony was great. What a beautiful occasion it was, unforgettable. I would say, it was one of the happiest moments in my life.

The positive energy was most definitely in the air. Everything seemed to be surely falling into place. I met this beautiful caramel complexioned woman while out in the city. I noticed she was breath taking at the very first glimpse. Her easy-going demeanor was the balance I needed. Could she be mine I was already wishing. I asked her out. I guess it was power in words and prayers. We instantly hit if off after a few dates.

Now you know everything well just about, there is
A "catch 22", so to speak. She had flour children ranging from the ages of one to six. Could it I handle this responsibility? At first it was something that sat heavily in my mind. After a while, it didn't matter. Just by spending a lot of time with them, I grew to love them. Being a single parent to four

Kids can be stressful. She was having a hard time molding a civilized, structure for them to be in. I know a lot of fellas probably would've been like "hell no" and kept it moving. Shit, the younger me would've said the same thing. You know what? I couldn't because I was in love. You see, being age twenty-six and having my prior experience gave me a mature element. A lot of men don't possess this state of mind typically until they're thirty-five to forty years of age.

I was ready to settle down and have more children. My "playa's card" has been officially turned in. I could be in a room full of women and none of them would strike my interest. My mind was set and I had made my decision. Outside of having multiple children, her mother was fighting cancer as well. I know many would say it had nothing to do with me but the human heart and love combats situations differently. So she had a lot on her plate. We couldn't go out much because of the responsibilities she had. I wanted to support her long the way.

As time went on, the mood kind of shifted. There was a slight resistance between her kid's father and me. It put her in the middle of the situation. Nothing pulled us apart; things mainly pulled us closer together. Over time I saw myself growing closer and closer to her. This individual had a warm spirit. In my eyes those who surrounded her, were taking her kindness for weakness. As many people often do to people of this world. We'd discuss these matters from time to time. I eventually started to stand up in her defense. Was I wrong? I might have been wrong some would say. Folks

(My fiancée and I at a O.E.S./Masonic Event '14)

trying to take advantage of my lady, the woman that I loved, well it wasn't going to happen on my watch. I really didn't care for a few of her friends, so that made her feel really uneasy. With all of that added to the list of issues our problems began to grow. Suddenly I started to become a hindrance. How could this happen? It's supposed to be her and me against the world.

She and I would argue ever other day. We would argue over the simplest things. You know at the time, I thought I was right, yeah maybe I could admit that I was being selfish. Even though my intentions were right, it seemed as if my actions spoke differently. Just thinking about it makes me tear up a little. I know it's because something that I adored could've bee lost. Love aint easy.

Being over ally cautious can tarnish a relationship. Things aren't going to be perfect. When the trust and the communication are active, everything will take its own course, and then there is no telling what road things will end up on.

The results will display according to how you play them out. I was afraid of falling from that "love high". I was afraid of losing it all. Many times males become control freaks, trying to over calculate the situation because, we are afraid of losing. It's not all about us. I was being overly protective of someone I cherish dearly. It seems I was trying so hard to prove that I'm not like the rest might have threw up several flags; I exaggerated things just a little.

Please take note this past winter wasn't the best ever. I almost lost my mind. Eighty percent of actions in life we bring them on ourselves. Let me explain the burden I was going through. The six people I wanted to see on Christmas were no where in sight. Just imagine having someone's attention at one point then being on the other side of the fence. Looking in the glass dome but nobody can hear you pecking. Well the just refuse to acknowledge you. I would text her, but I wouldn't get a response until hours later. I had lost my appetite and enthusiasm to do anything.

Wow! All I could think about was her. I wouldn't wish this feeling on my worst enemy. My heart had sank past the pit of my stomach I believe it to be somewhere under my feet being banged One of my homeboys mentioned that I should go to the club and get a replacement. I wasn't feeling that idea at all. The shit was written all over my face, I couldn't make it without my baby. Shit I was an emotional wreck. A few days after Christmas, she called me and invited me to bring the New Year in with her and the kids.

It was something that I wanted but I had an awkward feeling. I didn't know what to expect. Bringing up the past would've opened up wounds. So I went with the flow of things. Looking at her from the side gave me my reassurance of my feelings about this woman.

This was a lady that I loved without any strings attached. Without me having faith in Love I almost blew it all. I failed to realize it takes two and that we both had to let love be the mutual guide, we couldn't overshadow something so great with negative attitudes and influence. I didn't want anything from her but to see her smile. She deserves to see the finer things. I want everybody to know my lady is a strong woman. My love is the last of a dying breed. Her strength helped me recognize mine.

Chapter 13
Closing Scene

The time is now two o'clock am, on a Monday morning. I'm lying across the bed staring at a white box covered with a very thin layer of microfiber. What's inside of it beholds a white gold ½ caret engagement ring. I'm thinking to myself about all of things I've learned throughout the years. Flashes of moments pass in my mind. Destiny gives you no signs of what is to come. Nothing shows you the secrets to propel you here. The discovery of now is elusive. The thrills of it all so breathe taking. Who would have imagined?

I can't take back anything that happened in my past. All I know of my life is that I love hard, and I'm not ashamed to say it. The lack of affection I didn't receive from my mother made me a very strong individual. That taught me to guard my heart and show love to those who deserve it. I don't fault my mother nor discredit her. We all are adhesions from whatever situation we have been brought through whatever trails we fostered

Despite her flaws, my mother was the best mother she could be. My son's mother taught me the importance of patience, loyalty and family. I gained more insight within the short period of sharing my heart with her, than I had gained within an entire lifetime of loving. I appreciate her for being in my life and blessing me with a handsome son. He will be the foundation of a better me. Loving someone unconditionally is the completion of the love spectrum.

Nothing can persuade that state of mind because it is sealed with loyalty and passion. I can't believe that I'm at this point again. This time it feels right, my understandings are so much clearer and stronger. Earlier today I spoke with her father and he gave me his blessings. The advice that was given to me, by him will be treated as if it were to be a precious stone. I feel as if I have climbed a mountain and planted my flag with its families crest.

Well look at the irony in that. With my magazine company rising rapidly, I want her to be right by my side. As many people would compare being a power couple like Jay-Z & Beyonce' or T.I. & Tiny, I would rather we exceed that. Mainly because my love doesn't and wont have any limitations. There are a lot of books out that taint what love really is. People will always add money and sex to ingredients. They aren't part of the equation or formula.

I just want to give you all of the scoops, without the entire extra bullshit. This reading shall inspire you to desire love. One should elevate from every type of relationship you are involved in. Love is a beautiful thing if it's in the right hands. There's hope for the hopeless romantics. Just open your hands and hearts to be embraced by this energy. That God meant for us to share. Love is a virtue. Love is precious. Take care.

ABOUT THE AUTHOR

Derrick "June Garcia"(self proclaimed "Prince of the South") is an Atlanta based rap artist/entrepreneur with a lot of whit & character. His style and sound isn't your typical "ATL sound". His raspy voice, delivery and production, create the perfect image for his artistry. June's influences are T.I.P., Outkast, Snoop Dogg, Michael Jackson, 2Pac, B.o.B. & the list goes on.

In the beginning Mr. Garcia use to freestyle at lunchtime while in high school, battling the school's hottest M.C's. "Everyone one use to call me out, because I wasn't from the area. At first people use to poke fun but after awhile they accepted me because I would never let up with my barrage of lyrics and I didn't care what they thought about me." Just shortly after graduating from Bayside High School in (Virginia Beach, VA), Junes then girlfriend gave his demo to Keyon George (VMC). Keyon was an A&R for Teddy Riley.

CO-AUTHOR

Berlinda White first hit the scene in the late 90's on the poetry scene as Love X Love pronounced (Love times Love) she was known in many circles for having premonitions and having a very cognitive spirit. She felt something might be occurring that would be kind of dark so she began to pen her thoughts down in the poetry book "A Heaven in the Ghetto" where she did tributes to many people and many things in life. Her mother passed shortly after its release in 2007.

On her mothers deathbed she asked Berlinda to use the moniker L.A. in future works, because she knew her to be one of Life's Angels. Since then Berlinda has released, "Love for all Seasons" a poetry book and a compilation "Poetic Meter" and her gripping life story dealing with rape, incest and Life before being born on earth. In the gripping book "Leap from Heaven Journey to Earth". She was the host and Naked Conversations Radio on Blog Talk Radio and CEO of Naked Conversations media. She released the short film "Blues 101" this year. Later this year she is releasing the Novel "Sin".

Made in the USA
Columbia, SC
08 November 2021